A Crabtree Branches Book

By Kerri Mazzarella

CRABTREE
Publishing Company
www.crabtreebooks.com

School-to-Home Support for Caregivers and Teachers

This high-interest book is designed to motivate striving students with engaging topics while building fluency, vocabulary, and an interest in reading. Here are a few questions and activities to help the reader build upon his or her comprehension skills.

Before Reading:

- *What do I think this book is about?*
- *What do I know about this topic?*
- *What do I want to learn about this topic?*
- *Why am I reading this book?*

During Reading:

- *I wonder why...*
- *I'm curious to know...*
- *How is this like something I already know?*
- *What have I learned so far?*

After Reading:

- *What was the author trying to teach me?*
- *What are some details?*
- *How did the photographs and captions help me understand more?*
- *Read the book again and look for the vocabulary words.*
- *What questions do I still have?*

Extension Activities:

- *What was your favorite part of the book? Write a paragraph on it.*
- *Draw a picture of your favorite thing you learned from the book.*

TABLE OF
CONTENTS

WHERE TO FISH

Ice fishing is a form of freshwater fishing that takes place during winter months. It is the activity of catching fish with a line and hook that is dropped through a hole in the ice.

Ice fishing does not involve using a boat. However, some fishing spots that are off the grid will require a snowmobile to get to.

Ice fishing takes place on a frozen body of water such as a lake, pond, or stream. It is a little different than freshwater fishing but with the proper gear can be just as rewarding.

Ice fishing is enjoyed by **anglers** all over the world. If you enjoy icy weather this might be a fun hobby to try.

Ice fishing takes place in freezing locations. There are many popular ice fishing spots in Canada and the northern part of the U.S.

FUN FACTS

Lake of the Woods, Minnesota, is a popular place to try out ice fishing.

TYPES OF FISH

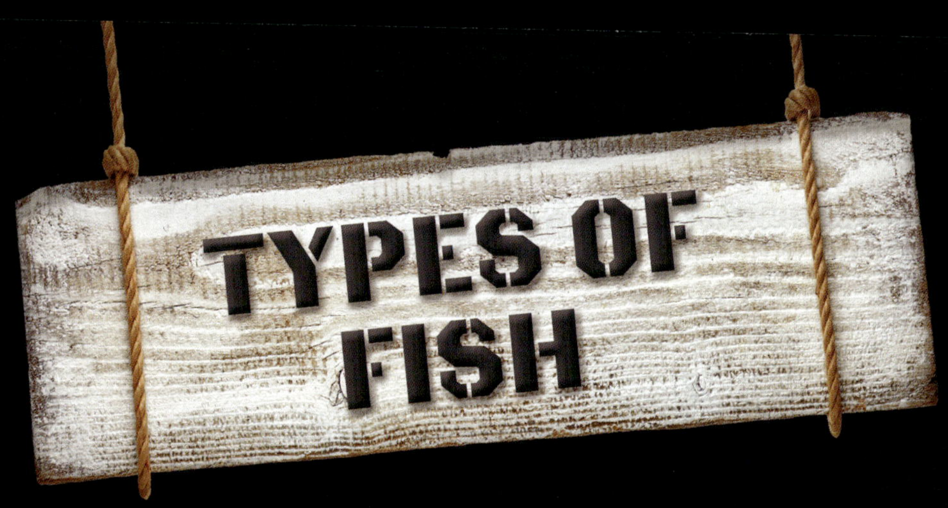

Many freshwater species of fish are caught ice fishing. Some include **walleye**, pike, and musky.

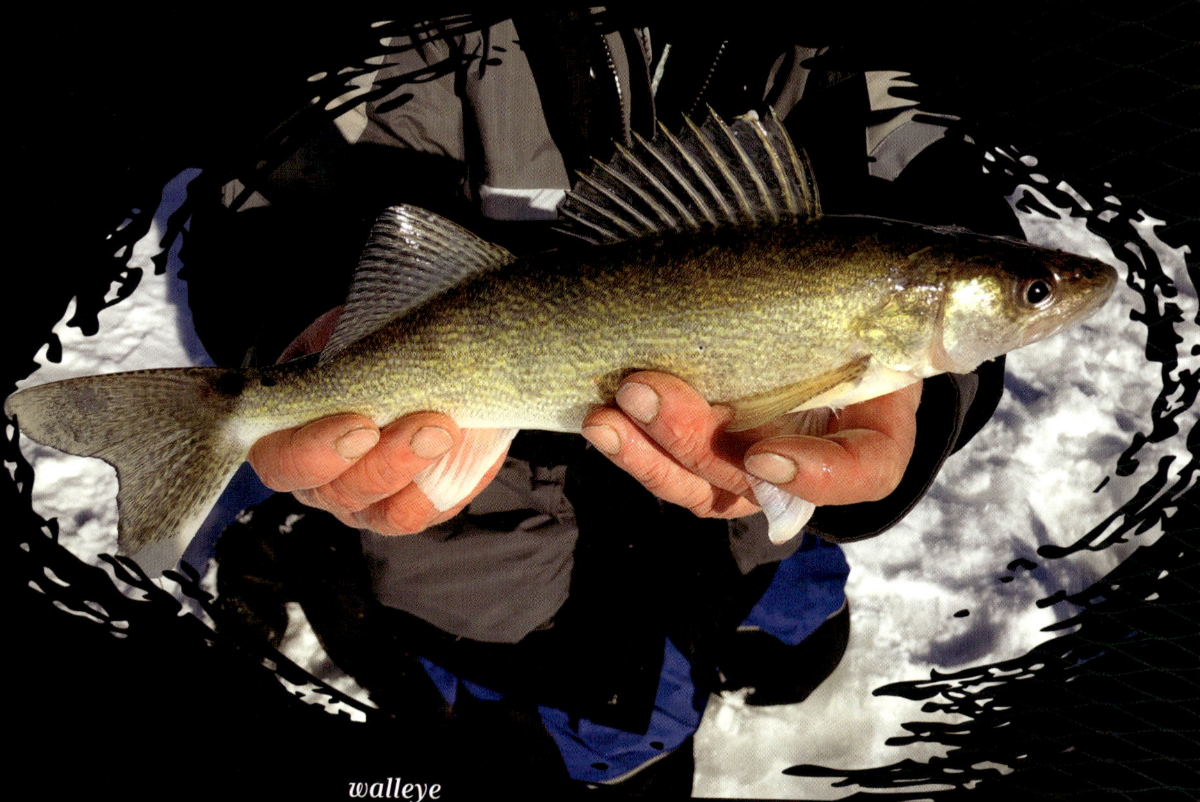

walleye

northern pike

Other fish caught include perch, panfish, trout, and bass. All of these fish are great to eat.

perch

trout

Fish in frozen lakes move slower in the winter and can be trickier to catch. Many anglers enjoy the challenge and are successful.

musky

FUN FACTS

The world's largest fish caught while ice fishing is a 53-inch (135 cm) musky in northwest Pennsylvania.

Some anglers ice fish to provide food for their family. Others enjoy the thrill of seeing what will be pulled out of the frozen lake.

SAFETY AND RULES

Ice fishing requires some precautions to stay safe. Remember to wear winter clothing to keep from getting **frostbite**.

It is strongly recommended to use the buddy system while ice fishing. A life jacket, first aid kit, and **ice picks** are also important things to have.

FUN FACTS

Special spikes can be worn on your boots to keep you from slipping while walking on the ice.

Take a good look at the ice. If the ice is dirty, wavy, or broken do not walk on it. Many people have fallen through ice, and this can be very dangerous.

You will need to purchase an ice fishing license. Be aware of seasonal regulations and size limitations for fish in your area. Each state and province has different rules.

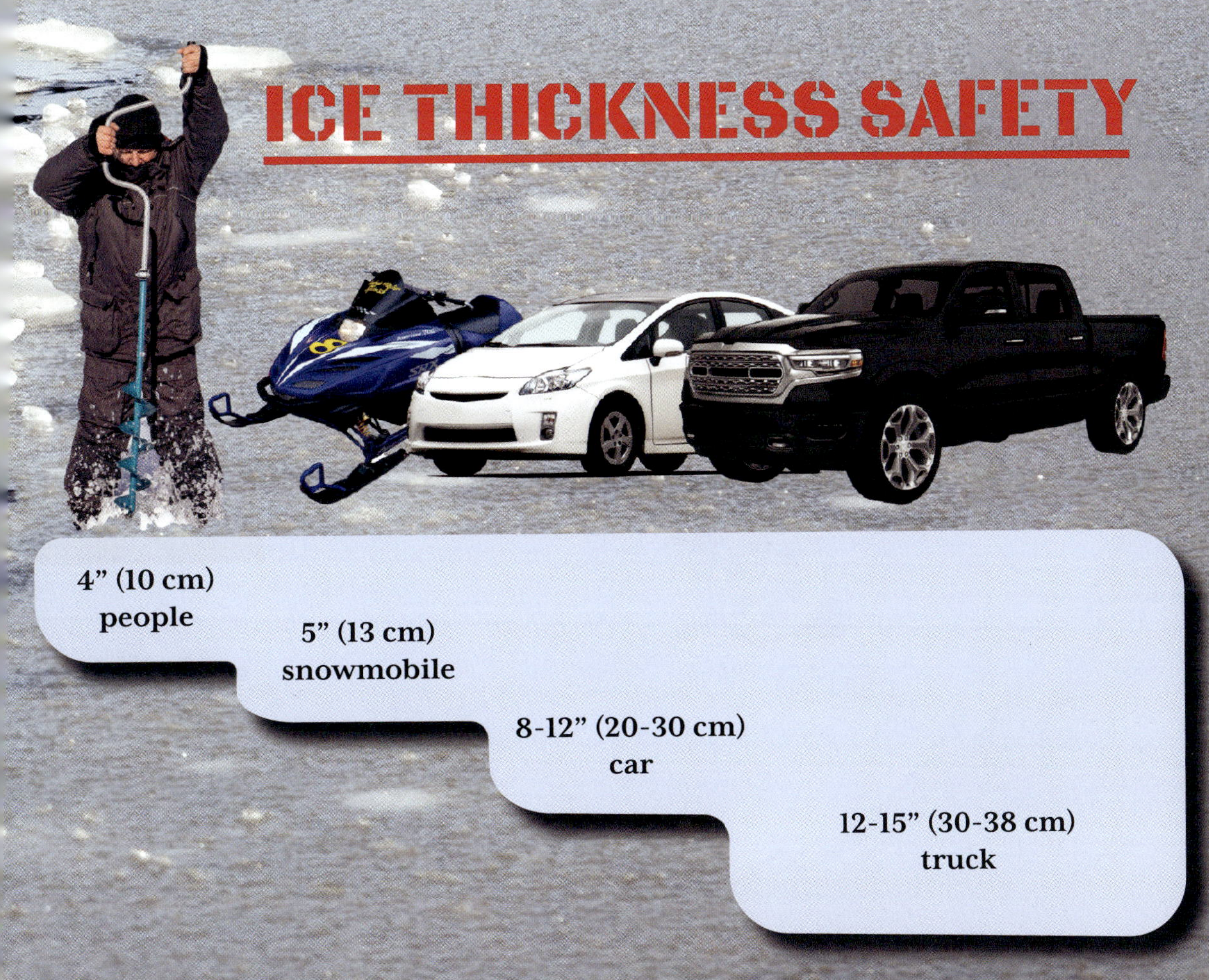

ICE THICKNESS SAFETY

4" (10 cm)
people

5" (13 cm)
snowmobile

8-12" (20-30 cm)
car

12-15" (30-38 cm)
truck

RODS AND EQUIPMENT

Ice fishing requires special equipment. An ice fishing rod is much shorter than a traditional one used in open water.

28 inches (71 cm) long

You can purchase an ice fishing rod and reel combo for around $50.

A **tip up** can be used instead of a rod. It contains a spool with line and a flag. When a fish bites the hook, it triggers the flag to pop up. Then you pull the line up by hand.

You can purchase a tip up and line for around $40.

An **ice auger** is used to drill a hole in the ice. The hole should measure between 8 and 10 inches (20 to 25 cm) depending on location.

An ice skimmer is used to scoop pieces of ice from the fishing hole.

FUN FACTS

An ice shanty is a small shelter that provides warmth during ice fishing. Some shanties are simple pop-up tents, and others are sturdier and require being dragged onto the ice by a vehicle.

WHAT'S IN YOUR TACKLE BOX?

You can purchase an ice fishing tackle kit for around $25 and tackle backpacks range from $25 to $80.

Most ice anglers have a tackle box. It is used to organize and store tackle and important gear.

Fishing hooks are the most important piece of tackle for every type of fishing. Hooks come in all shapes and sizes. Smaller hooks are used for ice fishing.

Two types of **bobbers** used in ice fishing are the spring bobber and the floating bobber.

Things you should have in your tackle box for ice fishing:

√ extra hooks

√ bobbers

√ weights

√ swivels

√ leader

√ knife

√ pliers

√ flashlight

√ extra line

√ jigs

√ spoons

√ lures

√ plastic bait

TYPES OF BAIT

Choosing bait for ice fishing is important. Both live and artificial bait can be used. Most bait and tackle stores can help you choose what is best for that area.

Some live bait used for ice fishing include **wax worms**, maggots, and minnows. The live bait is attached to the hook. Live bait is preferred by most beginner ice anglers.

wax worm

minnows

maggots

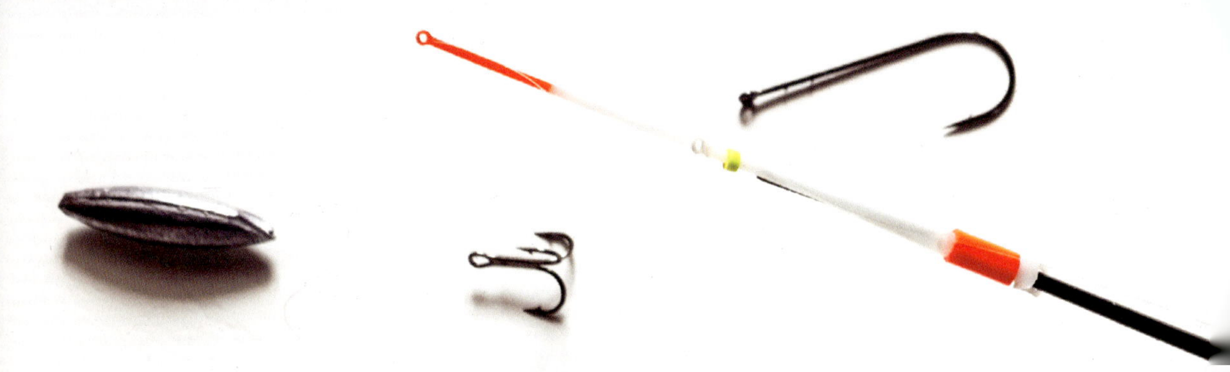

Artificial bait options for ice fishing are endless. **Spoons**, jigs, small lures, and small plastic worms are all great for ice fishing. They come in different colors, shapes, and sizes.

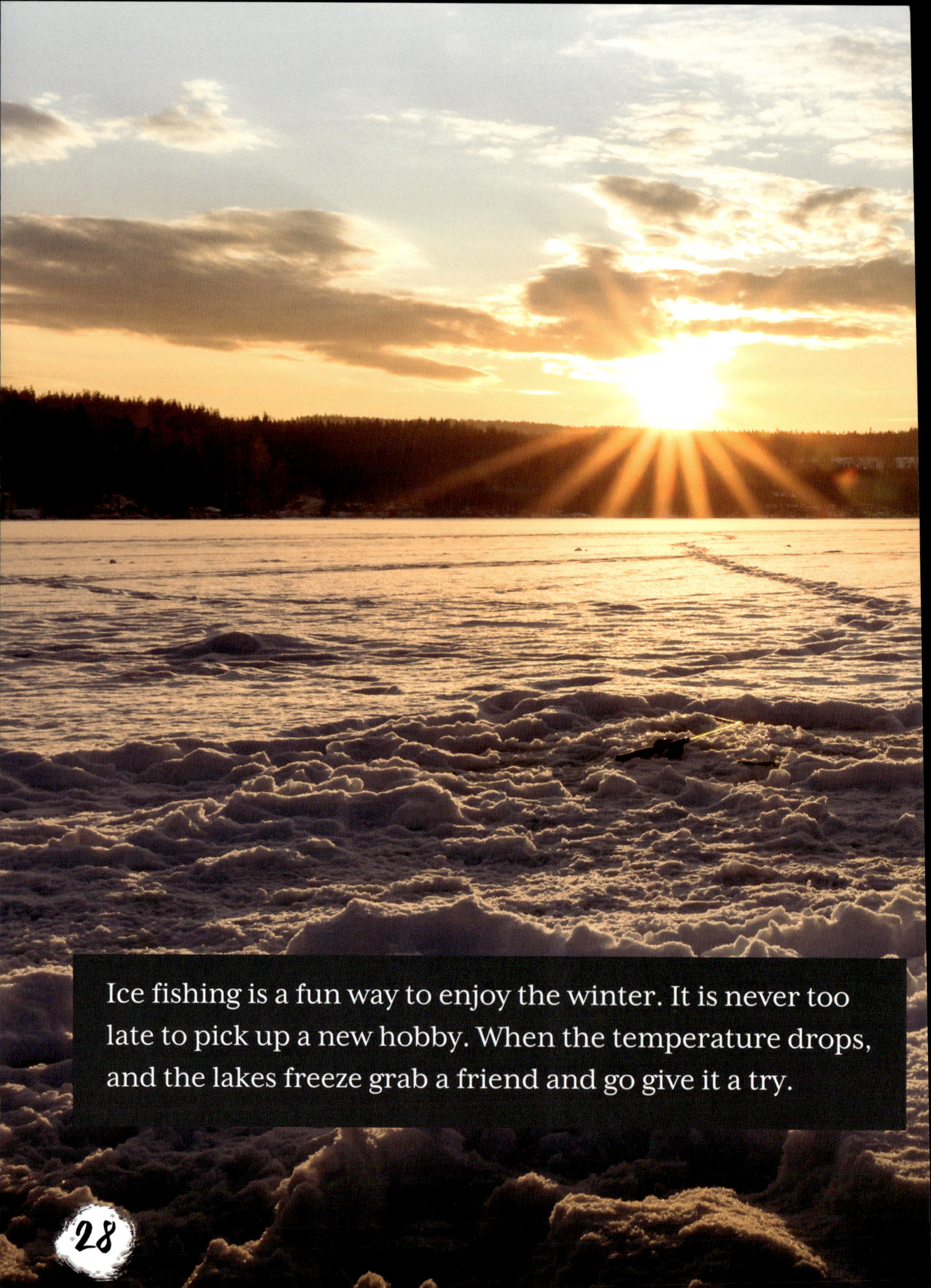

Ice fishing is a fun way to enjoy the winter. It is never too late to pick up a new hobby. When the temperature drops, and the lakes freeze grab a friend and go give it a try.

GLOSSARY

angler (ANG-gler): A person who fishes with a hook and line, especially for pleasure

bobbers (BOB-erz): Small floats placed on a fishing line to hold the hook at the desired depth

frostbite (FRAWST-bahyt): The freezing of a surface or deeper layer of tissue of some part of the body

ice auger (ahys AW-ger): A tool used for making large holes in ice for ice fishing

ice fishing (ahys FISH-ing): The activity of fishing through holes made in the ice of a frozen lake or river

ice pick (ahys pik): A hand tool ending in spikes used for gripping on to ice

spoons (spoonz): Shiny, curved metallic fishing lures

tip up (tip uhp): A device used in ice fishing in which a wire attached to a rod is tripped, raising a signal flag, when a fish takes the bait

walleye (WAWL-ahy): A large North American freshwater fish with large eyes

wax worm (waks wurm): A worm that is the larva of the wax moth

INDEX

WEBSITES TO VISIT

www.takemefishing.org/ice-fishing/ice-fishing-basics/ice-fishing-for-beginners/

https://fishingbooker.com/blog/ice-fishing-the-complete-illustrated-guide/

https://kids.kiddle.co/Ice_fishing

ABOUT THE AUTHOR

Kerri Mazzarella was raised on the east coast of southern Florida. She has enjoyed all types of fishing throughout her life. Her family spends the weekends on their boat catching fish in the river and ocean. Her four teenage children are all experienced anglers. Fish is often on the dinner menu at their house. She has never ice fished but hopes to try this winter.

Written by: Kerri Mazzarella
Designed by: Kathy Walsh
Proofreader: Crystal Sikkens

Photographs: Shutterstock; Cover: ©Maximillian cabinet, ©MicroOne, ©Zerbor, ©GreyMoth; Pg 3, 4, 8, 12, 16, 20, 24 © ESB professional; Pg 1, 3, 8, 10, 13, 16, 18, 20, 22, 24 © MicroOne; Pg 7, 10, 13, 19 ©Zerbor; Pg 4 ©CAmir Bajric; Pg 6 ©withGod; Pg 7 ©AJSTUDIO PHOTOGRAPHY; Pg 8 ©dcwcreations; Pg 9 ©Stephen Mcsweeny, ©Wawrzyniuk, ©Maximillian cabinet; Pg 10 ©M Huston; Pg 11 ©Denis Pepin; Pg 12 ©Dudarev MikhailPg 13 ©Birgit Reitz-Hofmann; Pg 14 ©FotoDuets; Pg 15 ©FedBul, © IgorXIII, ©Maksim Toome, ©Nerthuz; Pg 16 ©Maryna Pleshkun; Pg 17 ©Geoffrey Kuchera; Pg 18 ©Splingis; Pg 19 ©Luc Pouliot; Pg 20 ©Geoffrey Kuchera; Pg 21 ©Kondor83; Pg 22 ©Dan Thornberg; Pg 23 ©dasytnik; Pg 24 ©Eddie H S Cho; Pg 25 ©Zebek studio, ©Lost Mountain Studio, ©Little honey; Pg 27 © itakdalee; Pg 28 ©Marianne Danielsen

Library and Archives Canada Cataloguing in Publication
CIP available at Library and Archives Canada

Library of Congress Cataloging-in-Publication Data
CIP available at Library of Congress

Crabtree Publishing Company
www.crabtreebooks.com 1-800-387-7650

Printed in the USA/072022/CG20220201

Published in the United States Crabtree Publishing
347 Fifth Avenue, Suite 1402-145
New York, NY, 10016

Published in Canada Crabtree Publishing
616 Welland Ave.
St. Catharines, Ontario L2M 5V6